Practical
Karate

Fundamentals of Self-Defense

D1598869

Practical
Karate 1

*Fundamentals of
Self-Defense*

M. Nakayama
Donn F. Draeger

Tuttle Publishing
Boston • Rutland, Vermont • Tokyo

Copyright 1963 by Charles E. Tuttle Co., Inc. with editorial offices at
153 Milk Street, Boston, Massachusetts 02109.

Copyright © renewed 1991 by Charles E. Tuttle Co., Inc.

Library of Congress Catalog Card Number: 98-87646
ISBN 0-8048-0481-8

DISTRIBUTED BY

NORTH AMERICA
Tuttle Publishing
RR 1 Box 231-5
North Clarendon, VT 05759
Tel: (802) 773-8930
Tel: (800) 526-2778

SOUTHEAST ASIA
Berkeley Books Pte. Ltd.
5 Little Road #08-01
Singapore 536983
Tel: (65) 280-3320
Fax: (65) 280-6290

JAPAN
Tuttle Shokai Ltd.
1-21-13, Seki
Tama-ku, Kawasaki-shi
Kanagawa-ken 214, Japan
Tel: (044) 833-0225
Fax: (044) 822-0413

First edition
07 06 05 04 03 02 01   00 99 98   10 9 8 7 6 5 4 3 2 1

Printed in Singapore

TABLE OF CONTENTS

AUTHORS' FOREWORD

THERE IS, perhaps, no greater disservice to man than the creation of false confidence in his ability to defend himself. Whether this false confidence is manifested in his nations' armed might, or in his own personal ability, the result is the same, though of different proportions, when tested . . . DISASTER!

The current *karate* "boom" in the U.S.A. has instilled in many would-be "experts" a serious, false sense of security. This is the natural outgrowth of a human psychological weakness. Everyone wishes to be physically fit and able to defend himself and his loved ones from danger, and quickly turns to any sure-fire guarantee of such abilities.

Unscrupulous and unqualified self-appointed *karate* "experts" daily exploit this human weakness and prey on an innocent, unsuspecting public. This grossly perpetrated fraud is based on the quick learning of ancient mysterious Oriental combative forms such as *karate*, and almost always makes its appeal through colorful adjectives such as "super," "destructive," "terror tactics," and guarantees you mastery which will make you "fear no man." All such "get skillful quickly" schemes should be carefully investigated before choosing, for true *karate* involves constant dedication to training and is never a "short course" method. Choose your instructor carefully.

On the other hand, authentic teachers of *karate* do exist in the U.S.A., and their teachings have full merit. These teachings are deeply rooted in traditional, classical *karate* and require a liberal application of patience and regular training to develop expert *karate* skill. There are various schools which stem from historic Oriental antiquity, all of which are legitimate and have both merits and shortcomings. The choice of which school to follow can be decided only by the interested party.

The average person is confined to a daily life which requires of him a heavy investment in time and energy in order to earn a living. Leisure time is generally at a minimum and spent at less enervating pursuits than demanded by classical *karate* practice. But the need for a practical system of self-defense designed for the average person is more evident than ever before. Police files give mute testimony to the increasing number of robberies, assaults, and other vicious crimes.

In this book the necessary *karate* fundamentals are pictorially laid out in an easy, readable fashion. It is a book which in theory must preceed any actual ability with *karate* technique. Use it to build skills for efficient *karate* responses in self-defense situations. This will require some practice on your part: at least several times per week for short periods of time. When you have practiced all the movements described in this book and can perform them automatically, you will have a sound foundation on which to build self-defense skills. However, it is not necessary that you completely study and practice all the movements of this book before turning to the actual defense skills in volumes two, to six. You may "learn as you go," taking each self-defense situation in any order from the other books in this series, using this volume as a reference to the necessary skills which the self-defense response requires. Either way, you must practice.

The authors are indebted to the *Japan Karate Association,* Tokyo, Japan, for the use of their facilities and hereby acknowledge with pleasure the assistance of those members and officials who have made this book possible. Additional thanks is due to the excellent photographic skills of Akira Kasahara which has given this book its illustrations; to H. Shoji, an instructor of the *Japan Karate Association,* and to James S. Bregman, a student of combative arts whose posing for the "assailant" part of this text has been invaluable.

Tokyo, Japan

M. NAKAYAMA

DONN F. DRAEGER

8

PREFACE

KARATE is a martial art developed by people who were prohibited the use of weapons, thus making it a *defensive* art. When one is attacked, the empty hands (which the word *karate* implies) are quite sufficient to defend oneself if one is highly skilled in the art. However, to become highly skilled takes exacting discipline, both mental and physical. The main purpose of this series of four books is to avoid the advanced techniques of *karate* which require many years of study and instead to describe simplified *karate* technique as easy-to-learn responses to typical self-defense situations.

Karate is highly esteemed as a sport, self-defense, and as a physical attribute for athletics in general. It is becoming increasingly popular in schools, offices, factories, law enforcement agencies and the armed services, varying in degree as required by the respective wants and needs.

In response to the many requests for treatment of *karate* purely as a defensive system, it is hoped that the information contained in this series of six books will be more than sufficient to meet these requests. In conclusion, if readers of this series of books will fully understand the principles and ideals of *karate*, taking care to use its techniques with discretion, they will reflect great credit to this magnificent art.

Zentaro Kosaka
Former Foreign Minister
of Japan
Director, Japan Karate Association

9

THE FIRST and most complete and authoritative text on *karate* in the English language, titled *Karate: The Art of "Empty Hand" Fighting*, by Hidetaka Nishiyama and Richard C. Brown, instructor and member of the Japan Karate Association respectiely, made its appearance in 1960. It presents *karate* in its three main aspects—a healthful physical art, an exciting sport, and an effective form of self-defense. As such, it is considered the standard textbook of the Japan Karate Association and adequately serves both as a reference and in-structional manual for novice and expert alike.

Many students of *karate* find the study of classical *karate* somewhat impractical in modern Western society, chiefly because time limita-tions prohibit sufficient practice. These students generally desire to limit their interpretations of *karate* to self-defense aspects. With this sole training objective in mind, a series of six Books is being pre-pared which describes in simplified form, the necessary *karate* move-ments for personal defense that can be learned by anybody of average physical abilities.

The authors, M. Nakayama, Chief Instructor of the Japan Karate Association and Donn F. Draeger, a well-known instructor of com-bative arts, bring a balanced, practical, and functional approach to *karate,* based on the needs of Western society. As a specialized series of *karate* texts, these are authentic books giving full and minute ex-planations of the practical art of self-defense. All movements are per-formed in normal daily dress and bring the performer closer to reality.

Today, *karate* is attracting the attention of the whole world and is being popularized at an amazing rate. I sincerely hope that this series of books will be widely read as a useful reference for the lovers of *karate* all over the world. It is further hoped that the techniques shown in this series of books need never be used by any reader, but should an emergency arise making their use unavoidable, discretion in application should be the keynote.

M. Takagi

MASATOMO TAKAGI
Standing Director and
Head of the General Affairs
Department of the Japan
Karate Association

Practical
Karate

*Fundamentals of
Self-Defense*

ESSENTIAL POINTS

1. Never underestimate your assailant. Always assume he is dangerous.

2. Stepping, weight shifting, and body turning are the keys to avoiding an assailant's attack and bringing him into position for your counterattack.

3. Turn your body as a unit, not in isolated parts, for maximum effect.

4. If the ground is rough, bumpy, or slick, you may be unable to maneuver as you would like. Simple weight shifting and twisting of your hips may be all that is possible. Don't get too fancy in your footwork.

5. Your body can only act efficiently in *karate* techniques if you make it a stable foundation, working from braced feet and a balanced position as you deliver your blow.

6. Coordinate your blocking or striking action to the assailant's target area with your stepping, weight shifting, and body turning for maximum effect.

7. Do not oppose superior power with power, but seek to harmonize it with your body action and direct it to your advantage.

8. Seek to deliver your striking actions to the assailant's anatomical weak points (vital points) rather than to hard, resistant areas.

9. After delivering the striking action to your assailant's target area, you must never loose sight of him and you should be constantly alert for a continuation of his attack.

10. Use discretion in dealing out punishment to any assailant. Fit the degree of punishment to the situation.

Chapter One
THE SECRET WEAPONS:
Your Stances and Posture

CORRECT STANCES and postures are essential to effective *karate* techniques. They permit you to move quickly in order to avoid an assailant or to close with him to deliver a concentrated attack. As such, they should not be thought of as separate fundamentals, for they must work in harmony to produce effective *karate*. They are the foundation for all efficient *karate* movements and must be mastered.

Practice the stances and postures as often as you can. They must become automatic and "feel" comfortable. Remember: in a personal encounter you will not have time to think about which stance and posture is best. When you practice, a large mirror will aid you to check your form against that described in this chapter.

In your practice, do not allow yourself the convenience of a smooth surface to the exclusion of rough, wet, and slippery footings. Self-defense situations do not always take place on ideal surfaces. You must try the responses described in this book under all conditions if you are to be fully trained.

The following key points apply to the stances and postures:

1. Moving into a *karate* stance and posture from a normal body position such as walking or standing, requires SPEED. Practice frequently so that you can do this with a minimum of effort.
2. Movement must come from the HIPS. Do not start with your feet and leave your body "behind."
3. Keep your body BALANCED. Keep your hips level and body perpendicular to the ground.
4. Practice both RIGHT and LEFT stances and postures. Don't develop a "sugar" side.

Changing Direction: The Forward Stance with Front-facing Posture is used to close with an assailant in order to block side attacks as well as to counterattack forward.

Step forward to the side by pivoting inward on one foot and advancing the other leg to the side, a distance of about twice the width of your shoulders and 30° to the side. Brace

Stepping In: The Forward Stance with Front-facing Posture is used to close with an assailant in order to block frontal and side attacks as well as to counterattack forward.

Advance one leg about twice the width of the shoulders and 30° to the side. Brace rear leg in a fully extended position. Front leg is bent with the knee just over the toe, toe pointed slightly inward. Keep both heels on the ground. Center weight with 60% on the front leg. The Half-front-facing Posture may also be used (not shown).

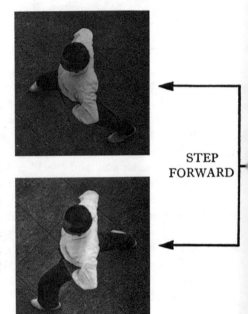

STEP
FORWARD

TOP VIEW

14

rear leg in a fully extended position so that the front leg is bent with the knee just over the toe, toe turned slightly inward. Keep both heels on the ground. Center weight so that 60% is on the front leg (see left). The Half-front-facing Posture may also be used (not shown).

PIVOT
and
TURN

STEP
BACK

PIVOT
and
TURN

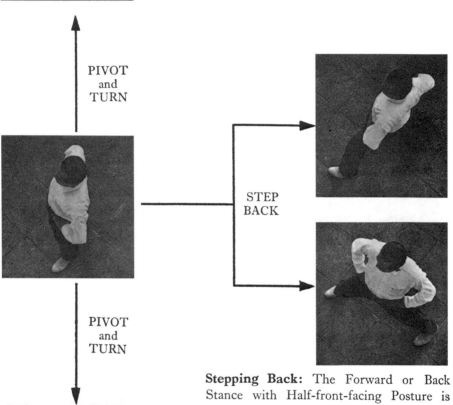

Stepping Back: The Forward or Back Stance with Half-front-facing Posture is used to avoid and block frontal and side attacks and to counterattack. Back Stance is useful in delivering frontal kicking attacks.

Retreat one leg a distance of about twice the width of the shoulders and 30° to the side. Brace rear leg in a fully extended position. Front leg is bent with knee just over the toe, toe turned slightly inward. Keep heels on the ground. Center weight with 60% on front leg. This is the Forward Stance.

Back Stance: Bend rear leg and shift about 70% of weight onto this leg, pointing toes (rear foot) outward at a right angle to front foot. The Front-facing Posture may also be used with either the Back Stance (top two pictures only) and the Forward Stance.

BACK STANCE
(half-front facing)

STEP and PIVOT
(front-facing)

FRONT VIEW

BACK STANCE
(half-front facing)

STEP BACK

STEP and PIVOT
(front-facing)

STEP FORWARD

(front-facing)

17

BEGINNING
stance and posture

Stance and Posture Exercise: You will find this exercise helpful in developing the efficient stances and postures required in performing the *karate* responses described in this book. Practice it frequently. A few minutes each day or several times a week will be sufficient.

Stand in the Forward Stance.

Keep your feet in place, braced to afford a stable base for movement.

Twist your whole upper body as a unit, not in isolated parts.

Keep your hips level and your body perpendicular to the ground as you twist.

Twist as shown in the pictures, passing through the Half-front-facing Posture to the Front-facing Posture and return for twenty repetitions. Repeat on the other side from a Forward Stance taken to that side.

half-front-facing
forward stance

front-facing
forward stance

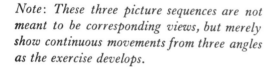

Note: These three picture sequences are not meant to be corresponding views, but merely show continuous movements from three angles as the exercise develops.

Remember these

ESSENTIAL POINTS

1. Never underestimate your assailant. Always assume he is dangerous.

2. Stepping, weight shifting, and body turning are the keys to avoiding an assailant's attack and bringing him into position for your counterattack.

3. Turn your body as a unit, not in isolated parts, for maximum effect.

4. If the ground is rough, bumpy, or slick, you may be unable to maneuver as you would like. Simple weight shifting and twisting of your hips may be all that is possible. Don't get too fancy in your footwork.

5. Your body can only act efficiently in *karate* techniques if you make it a stable foundation, working from braced feet and a balanced position as you deliver your blow.

6. Coordinate your blocking or striking action to the assailant's target area with your stepping, weight shifting, and body turning for maximum effect.

7. Do not oppose superior power with power, but seek to harmonize it with your body action and direct it to your advantage.

8. Seek to deliver your striking actions to the assailant's anatomical weak points (vital points) rather than to hard, resistant areas.

9. After delivering the striking action to your assailant's target area, you must never loose sight of him and you should be constantly alert for a continuation of his attack.

10. Use discretion in dealing out punishment to any assailant. Fit the degree of punishment to the situation.

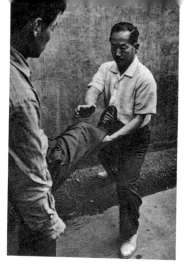

Chapter Two
AVOIDING THE ATTACK:
Your Blocking Actions

IN A PERSONAL encounter, your *first* responsibility is to avoid your assailant's attack. *If you do nothing else,* you must successfully avoid his action. Your most practiced and best *karate* technique will be of little or no value if the assailant " connects."

Avoiding an assailant's attack does not mean that you merely become a "punching bag" for him. Rather, it means that you take the appropriate steps to put a stop to his aggressive actions. Avoiding an assailant in *karate* style can be done in various ways, but all methods are based on the fundamentals of stance and posture described in Chapter 1, the key to your *karate* success.

In addition, avoiding an assailant requires you to learn how to dodge and shift your body by stepping, sliding, turning, and combining these movements with parrying and blocking actions which deflect an assailant's attack and open him to your *karate* counterattack. Your complete safety in self-defense situations depends almost entirely upon your ability to avoid your assailant. For that reason, you must practice avoiding movements described in this chapter until you are confident that you can perform them automatically. A large mirror will aid you to spot-check your form. Make all these movements lightly and quickly. Always concentrate on proper form which will ensure good balance and eventually permit speedy action.

Using the elements of avoiding an assailant—stance, posture, body movement, and parry-blocking action—comprises five methods. These are:

1. A well-placed, very hard blocking action causing intense pain to the assailant which discourages him from further assault.

2. A well-placed but moderate parry-blocking action which misdirects the assailant's force and unbalances him.

3. A well-placed parry-blocking action followed simultaneously by a proper *karate* counterattack.

4. Body movement alone (no parry-blocking action) to avoid the assailant's attack and simultaneous counterattack in proper *karate* fashion.

5. A *karate* attack before the assailant's attack can fully materialize, thus "beating him to the punch."

The Rising Block: Used to block an attack to the face, this action should be performed from a Forward Stance with the body in a Front or Half-front-facing Posture. Either arm may be used.

Perform the Rising Block on the side of the advanced foot which bears about 60% of your weight. Feet are braced with heels on the ground. Swing arm upward and slightly forward with elbow bent more than 90.° Keeping it close to the body as it rises, twist the arm so that the thumb points downward, then snap arm upward against assailant's striking arm at any point below his elbow. Use the outer, bony edge of the wrist as point of contact, centered on the

vertical line of the body. Note that the elbow should not be raised higher than the hand and that the elbow falls within a vertical line at the side of your body. Simultaneous with this blocking action, the other hand is made into a tightly clenched fist and withdrawn close alongside the body, twisting the palm upward at the hip, thus making it ready for a counterattack. Tense chest muscles as you strike with the Rising Block. (See pictures on these two pages.)

The Rising Block can be used effectively by stepping slightly to the side as shown above. This action is one of additional evasion and necessary in cases where you expect a kicking attack to follow the assailant's punch.

The Rising Block can be used effectively by stepping directly into the assailant as shown above. This action is one which permits close range counterattack.

26

The Forearm Block: Used to block an attack to the solar plexus or higher, this action should be performed from a Forward Stance with the body in a Front or Half-front-facing Posture. Either arm may be used. Blocking action can be directed against the inside or outside of an assailant's attacking arm.

27

Perform the Forearm Block on the side of the advanced foot which bears about 60% of your weight. Feet are braced with heels on the ground. The Forearm Block to the inside is shown in the four pictures above, and to the outside in the pictures below. They are performed identically. Swing the arm from the side in a half circle, keeping a tightly clenched fist and the elbow bent slightly less than 90°, to a point against the assailant's striking arm, anywhere below his elbow. As you swing the arm to block, twist the arm so that the palm faces you at the

strike. The outer, bony edge of the wrist makes contact with the target in a snapping fashion and centers on the vertical plane of the body. Simultaneous with this blocking action, the other hand is made into a tightly clenched fist and withdrawn close alongside the body, twisting the palm upward at the hip, making it ready for a counterattack. Tense chest muscles as you strike with the Forearm Block. Notice the twist of the hips with the blocking action.

Memorize these

ESSENTIAL POINTS

1. Never underestimate your assailant. Always assume he is dangerous.

2. Stepping, weight shifting, and body turning are the keys to avoiding an assailant's attack and bringing him into position for your counterattack.

3. Turn your body as a unit, not in isolated parts, for maximum effect.

4. If the ground is rough, bumpy, or slick, you may be unable to maneuver as you would like. Simple weight shifting and twisting of your hips may be all that is possible. Don't get too fancy in your footwork.

5. Your body can only act efficiently in *karate* techniques if you make it a stable foundation, working from braced feet and a balanced position as you deliver your blow.

6. Coordinate your blocking or striking action to the assailant's target area with your stepping, weight shifting, and body turning for maximum effect.

7. Do not oppose superior power with power, but seek to harmonize it with your body action and direct it to your advantage.

8. Seek to deliver your striking actions to the assailant's anatomical weak points (vital points) rather than to hard, resistant areas.

9. After delivering the striking action to your assailant's target area, you must never loose sight of him and you should be constantly alert for a continuation of his attack.

10. Use discretion in dealing out punishment to any assailant. Fit the degree of punishment to the situation.

The Knife-hand Block: Used to block an attack to the solar plexus or higher, this action should be performed from a Forward or Back Stance with the body in a Half-front-facing Posture. Either arm may be used. Blocking action can be directed against the inside or outside of an assailant's attacking arm.

Perform the Knife-hand Block on the side of the advanced foot which bears about 30% of your weight. Feet are braced with heels on the ground. Pictures at the left show the Knife-hand Block directed against the outside of the assailant's attacking arm. The blocking hand begins from a position beside the opposite ear, thumb up. Keep fingers together, held in position by the thumb folded and clamped tightly against the base of the forefinger. (See page 70.) Slash the blocking hand diagonally downward and forward with the elbow as a pivot point, against the assailant's striking arm anywhere below his elbow.

As you slash, twist the arm at the strike, so that the palm faces down and away from you, the outer edge of the heel of the hand making contact with the target in a snapping fashion and centering on the vertical line of the body. During this slashing action, take care not to bend the wrist or straighten the arm too much. Cut diagonally downward in a straight line from the ear to the target. Simultaneous with this blocking action, the other arm, hand fashioned similarly, is withdrawn close to the body to a position in front of the middle chest, twisting the palm upward as you go. Tense chest muscles as you strike with the Knife-hand Block.

Have you learned these?

ESSENTIAL POINTS

1. Never underestimate your assailant. Always assume he is dangerous.

2. Stepping, weight shifting, and body turning are the keys to avoiding an assailant's attack and bringing him into position for your counterattack.

3. Turn your body as a unit, not in isolated parts, for maximum effect.

4. If the ground is rough, bumpy, or slick, you may be unable to maneuver as you would like. Simple weight shifting and twisting of your hips may be all that is possible. Don't get too fancy in your footwork.

5. Your body can only act efficiently in *karate* techniques if you make it a stable foundation, working from braced feet and a balanced position as you deliver your blow.

6. Coordinate your blocking or striking action to the assailant's target area with your stepping, weight shifting, and body turning for maximum effect.

7. Do not oppose superior power with power, but seek to harmonize it with your body action and direct it to your advantage.

8. Seek to deliver your striking actions to the assailant's anatomical weak points (vital points) rather than to hard, resistant areas.

9. After delivering the striking action to your assailant's target area, you must never loose sight of him and you should be constantly alert for a continuation of his attack.

10. Use discretion in dealing out punishment to any assailant. Fit the degree of punishment to the situation.

The Grasping Block: Used to block an attack to the solar plexus and higher and to unbalance the assailant, this action should be performed from a Forward Stance with the body in a Front or Half-front-facing posture. Both arms are used in a coordinated fashion and are best directed against the outside of an assailant's attacking arm.

35

Perform the Grasping Block on the side of the advanced foot which bears about 60% of your weight. Feet are braced with heels on the ground. Pictures on these two pages show the Grasping Block directed against the outside of an assailant's successively punching arms. Sweep hands together from the side, directing them against the outside of the assailant's striking arm in one of two fashions. In the four above pictures, the outermost hand pushes against the assailant's striking arm from the side at a point just above his elbow, while the innermost hand grasps the assailant on top of his wrist. This double hand action of push and grasp should be done with the thumbs pointing at each other as

shown in the upper right picture. As contact is made with the assailant's arm, both hands must pull in the direction of the rearmost foot. In the four pictures below, the innermost hand pushes against the assailant's striking arm from the side at a point just above his elbow, keeping the thumb pointing downward. The outermost hand crosses over the other hand, grasping the assailant's striking arm at the wrist from the top. The thumb points to the rear. This double hand action of push and grasp should be done as shown in the two lower pictures on this page. As contact is made with the assailant's arm, both hands pull in the direction of the rearmost foot. Notice the twist of the hips with this pulling action.

Do not forget these

ESSENTIAL POINTS

1. Never underestimate your assailant. Always assume he is danger-
    ous.

2. Stepping, weight shifting, and body turning are the keys to avoid-
    ing an assailant's attack and bringing him into position for your
    counterattack.

3. Turn your body as a unit, not in isolated parts, for maximum
    effect.

4. If the ground is rough, bumpy, or slick, you may be unable to
    maneuver as you would like. Simple weight shifting and twisting
    of your hips may be all that is possible. Don't get too fancy in
    your footwork.

5. Your body can only act efficiently in *karate* techniques if you make
    it a stable foundation, working from braced feet and a balanced
    position as you deliver your blow.

6. Coordinate your blocking or striking action to the assailant's target
    area with your stepping, weight shifting, and body turning for
    maximum effect.

7. Do not oppose superior power with power, but seek to harmonize
    it with your body action and direct it to your advantage.

8. Seek to deliver your striking actions to the assailant's anatomical
    weak points (vital points) rather than to hard, resistant areas.

9. After delivering the striking action to your assailant's target area,
    you must never loose sight of him and you should be constantly
    alert for a continuation of his attack.

10. Use discretion in dealing out punishment to any assailant. Fit the
    degree of punishment to the situation.

The Wedge Block: Used to block an attack to the face in which the assailant is using his hands and arms as if he were double neck or lapel grasping. This block misdirects the assailant's attack and creates openings for a swift counterattack. This action should be performed from the Forward or Back Stance with Front-facing Posture. Blocking action can utilize either open or closed hands and is directed against the inside of the assailant's simultaneously attacking arms.

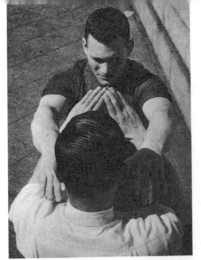

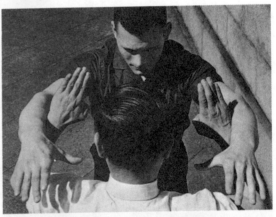

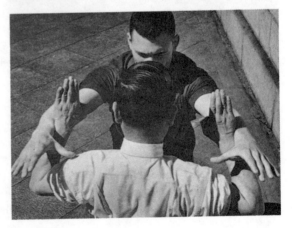

Perform the Wedge Block from a solid stance, either the Forward Stance (about 60% of your weight on the advanced foot) or the Back Stance (about 70% of your weight on the rear foot). Maintain a Front-facing Posture. Feet are braced with heels on the ground. Pictures to the left show the Wedge Block directed upward against a choking attack. Drive both arms upward while formed like a triangular wedge, with the hands acting as the vertex of the triangle, between the assailant's attacking arms. Either an open hand or a closed fist may be used for this action (open hand shown). Holding the hands together, direct the outer bony edges of the wrists and forearms hard against the assailant's inner arms at any point between his wrist and elbow (upper two pictures).

As the assailant's attacking arms are misdirected, snap your arms outward against the inner surfaces of the assailant's arms, keeping your arms bent and tensing your chest muscles (lower picture).

It is well to anticipate a kicking or kneeing attack by the assailant in this situation. When performing the Wedge Block, great care must be taken to guard against a kick in the groin. If the misdirecting and spreading action shown in the lower picture is maintained, the assailant is unbalanced and his kicking or kneeing attack is thus weakened enough to render it ineffective.

Review once more these

ESSENTIAL POINTS

1. Never underestimate your assailant. Always assume he is dangerous.

2. Stepping, weight shifting, and body turning are the keys to avoiding an assailant's attack and bringing him into position for your counterattack.

3. Turn your body as a unit, not in isolated parts, for maximum effect.

4. If the ground is rough, bumpy, or slick, you may be unable to maneuver as you would like. Simple weight shifting and twisting of your hips may be all that is possible. Don't get too fancy in your footwork.

5. Your body can only act efficiently in *karate* techniques if you make it a stable foundation, working from braced feet and a balanced position as you deliver your blow.

6. Coordinate your blocking or striking action to the assailant's target area with your stepping, weight shifting, and body turning for maximum effect.

7. Do not oppose superior power with power, but seek to harmonize it with your body action and direct it to your advantage.

8. Seek to deliver your striking actions to the assailant's anatomical weak points (vital points) rather than to hard, resistant areas.

9. After delivering the striking action to your assailant's target area, you must never loose sight of him and you should be constantly alert for a continuation of his attack.

10. Use discretion in dealing out punishment to any assailant. Fit the degree of punishment to the situation.

SWEEPING BLOCK
(below)

PRESSING BLOCK
(page 45)

PALM-HEEL BLOCK
(page 46)

The Sweeping Block: Used to block an attack to the face by sweeping the assailant's attack aside and creating an opening for a counter-attack. Performed from a Forward Stance with the body in a Front or Half-front-facing Posture. Either arm may be used. Blocking action can be directed against the inside or outside of an assailant's attacking arm.

Perform the Sweeping Block on the side of the advanced foot, bearing about 60% of your weight. Feet are braced with heels on the ground. The pictures show the Sweeping Block to the inside and the outside of the assailant's attacking arm. Swing the arm from the side in a short arc with hand open, fingers together and held in position by the thumb folded and clamped tightly against the base of the forefinger. Keeping the elbow bent, snap the palm, wrist, or the knife edge of the blocking hand hard against the assailant's attacking arm at any point near his wrist. Sweep his attack in the direction of your rearmost leg. Notice twist of the hips during this sweeping action. Simultaneous with this sweeping and twisting, withdraw the other arm close alongside the body, twisting palm upward, hand clenched in a tight fist at the hip, thus making it ready for counterattack.

44

The Pressing Block: Used to block an attack to the groin or abdominal regions by holding the assailant's attacking member in place while you deliver a simultaneous counterattack. Performed from a Forward Stance in a Front or Half-front-facing Posture. Either arm may be used. Blocking action is generally directed downward and forward against the top of the assailant's attacking arm.

Perform the Pressing Block on the side of the advanced foot, bearing about 60% of your weight. Feet are braced with heels on the ground. The Pressing Block is shown in the picture. Drive the arm with elbow bent slightly more than 90°, hand held in a tightly clenched fist, hard forward and slightly downward against the assailant's attacking arm at any point along his arm from biceps to wrist. Use the outer edge of the blocking arm along the bony area of the wrist and forearm as the point of contact. Simultaneous with this forward-downward pressing action, withdraw the other arm close alongside the body, twisting palm upward, hand clenched in a tight fist at the hip, thus making it ready for a counterattack. Hips may twist to aid this movement. Tense chest muscles as you block.

The Palm-heel Block: Used to block an attack to areas from the groin region upward, this action should be performed from a Forward Stance with the body in a Front or Half-front-facing Posture. Either arm may be used. Blocking action should be limited to the top or the side of the assailant's attacking arm.

Perform the Palm-heel Block on the side of the advanced foot which bears about 60% of your weight. Feet are braced with heels on the ground. Left picture shows the Palm-heel Block applied against the top of the assailant's striking arm. Thrust the arm forward and downward in a straight line—snapping the wrist by flexing it nearly to a right angle, palm forward, fingers curled downward at the second joints—as you reach the limit of arm extension. (See page 70.) Using the heel of the hand as a contact point, snap it hard against the top of the assailant's attacking arm at any point along his forearm. Simultaneously, withdraw the other arm close alongside the body, twisting palm upward, hand clenched in a tight fist at the hip, thus making ready for a counterattack. Hips may twist to aid this blocking action. Notice that the block is directly in front of the vertical line of the body.

Right picture shows the Palm-heel Block applied against the side of the assailant's striking arm. This action is similar to the Palm-heel Block applied to the top of the assailant's attacking arm, but the arm thrust is delivered more or less parallel to the ground and brought hard against the assailant's forearm from the side. Tense chest muscles as you block. (See pictures, page 80.)

46

The X-block: Used to block an attack to the head or abdominal-groin regions, this action should be performed from a Forward Stance with the body in a Front or Half-front-facing Posture. Both arms are used in a coordinated fashion and this blocking action may be directed either upward or downward.

Perform the X-block from a solid stance with about 60% of your weight on the advanced foot. Feet are braced with heels on the ground. Pictures on this page show the X-block directed upward against an attack to the face. Thrust both hands (normally left in front of right if right-handed) forward and upward in a straight line, with fists tightly clenched. Direct the arms against the underside of the assailant's striking arm at any point near his wrist, wedging his arm in the saddle formed by the cross of the arms. Continue driving upward to a point no higher than the top of your head. Notice that the X-block is about one foot in front of your head and that the elbows are not projecting beyond the sides of the body. Pic-

tures on this page show the X-block directed downward against a kicking attack to the groin or abdominal regions. Thrust both hands (normally right hand on top of left if right-handed) forward and downward in a straight line, fists clenched tightly. Direct them against the upperside of the assailant's kicking leg at any point along his shin, wedging his leg in the saddle formed by the cross of your arms. Continue driving the X-block downward until you have fully extended your arms. Note that the completed block is about one foot in front of the mid-body region and that the upper part of the body is not leaning forward. The elbows do not project beyond the sides of the body. Tense chest muscles as you block.

49

Do not underestimate these

ESSENTIAL POINTS

1. Never underestimate your assailant. Always assume he is dangerous.

2. Stepping, weight shifting, and body turning are the keys to avoiding an assailant's attack and bringing him into position for your counterattack.

3. Turn your body as a unit, not in isolated parts, for maximum effect.

4. If the ground is rough, bumpy, or slick, you may be unable to maneuver as you would like. Simple weight shifting and twisting of your hips may be all that is possible. Don't get too fancy in your footwork.

5. Your body can only act efficiently in *karate* techniques if you make it a stable foundation, working from braced feet and a balanced position as you deliver your blow.

6. Coordinate your blocking or striking action to the assailant's target area with your stepping, weight shifting, and body turning for maximum effect.

7. Do not oppose superior power with power, but seek to harmonize it with your body action and direct it to your advantage.

8. Seek to deliver your striking actions to the assailant's anatomical weak points (vital points) rather than to hard, resistant areas.

9. After delivering the striking action to your assailant's target area, you must never loose sight of him and you should be constantly alert for a continuation of his attack.

10. Use discretion in dealing out punishment to any assailant. Fit the degree of punishment to the situation.

The Downward Block: Used to block an attack to the groin or abdomen by stopping or deflecting the force of an assailant's attack and creating an opening for a counterattack. Performed from a Forward Stance with the body in a Front or Half-front-facing Posture. Either arm may be used. Blocking action may be directed against the inside or the outside of an assailant's attacking member. Though not strictly limited to kicking attacks, this method of blocking is effectively used against them.

Perform the Downward Block on the side of the advanced foot which bears about 60% of your weight. Feet are braced with heels on the ground. The Downward Block to the inside of an attacking leg is shown in the pictures on this page. The blocking arm is folded across the body with that fist near the opposite ear, palm facing inward. The other arm is held, fist tightly clenched, in front of the body. Swing the fist of the blocking arm diagonally downward, twisting the arm so that the back of the hand is uppermost as the blocking arm reaches its full extension. Strike hard against any convenient part of

the assailant's leg, such as the inner ankle or shin bone, using the outer surface of the forearm near the wrist as the point of contact. As you swing the blocking arm downward, simultaneously withdraw the other arm close alongside the body, twisting the palm upward, hand in a tightly clenched fist at the hip, thus making it ready for a counterattack. Tense chest muscles as you strike with the Downward Block. Pictures on this page show this blocking action to the outside of the assailant's kicking attack. Perform it similarly as you did for the inside blocking action. Tense chest muscles as you block.

Your last chance to learn these

ESSENTIAL POINTS

1. Never underestimate your assailant. Always assume he is dangerous.

2. Stepping, weight shifting, and body turning are the keys to avoiding an assailant's attack and bringing him into position for your counterattack.

3. Turn your body as a unit, not in isolated parts, for maximum effect.

4. If the ground is rough, bumpy, or slick, you may be unable to maneuver as you would like. Simple weight shifting and twisting of your hips may be all that is possible. Don't get too fancy in your footwork.

5. Your body can only act efficiently in *karate* techniques if you make it a stable foundation, working from braced feet and a balanced position as you deliver your blow.

6. Coordinate your blocking or striking action to the assailant's target area with your stepping, weight shifting, and body turning for maximum effect.

7. Do not oppose superior power with power, but seek to harmonize it with your body action and direct it to your advantage.

8. Seek to deliver your striking actions to the assailant's anatomical weak points (vital points) rather than to hard, resistant areas.

9. After delivering the striking action to your assailant's target area, you must never loose sight of him and you should be constantly alert for a continuation of his attack.

10. Use discretion in dealing out punishment to any assailant. Fit the degree of punishment to the situation.

The Scooping Block: Used to block kicking actions to the groin or abdominal regions and to break the assailant's balance to create an opening for a counterattack. Performed from a Forward Stance with the body in a Front or Half-front-facing Posture. Both arms are used in a coordinated fashion and are best directed from inside the assailant's kicking leg.

Perform the Scooping Block on the side of the advanced leg which bears about 60% of your weight. Feet are braced with heels on the ground. The Scooping Block to the inside of an attacking leg is shown in the above pictures. As the assailant kicks at you, your catch hand, operating from the outside of the assailant's leg, makes a quick circular motion and scoops the assailant's leg slightly upward and in the direction of the kick by grasping his ankle in a cupping fashion. The other hand thrusts downward on a diagonal, hard against the assailant's knee, slightly from the inside. As contact is made with this thrust, the body is twisted in the direction of the thrust to increase its effect. Tense chest muscles as you contact the assailant's knee with the thrust hand.

The pictures on this page show the Scooping Block from another angle which better clarifies the thrusting action.

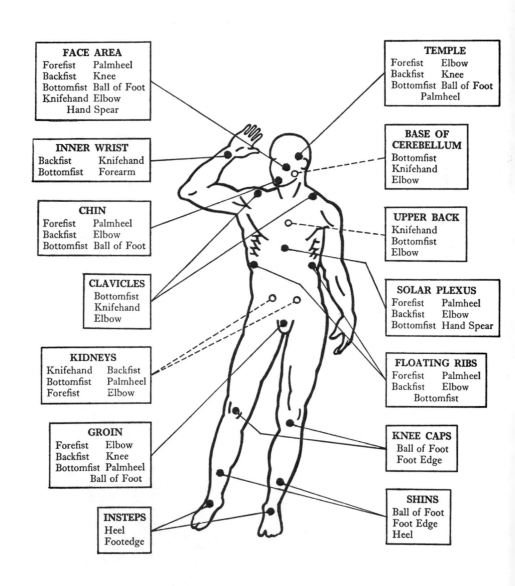

FACE AREA

Forefist   Palmheel
Backfist   Knee
Bottomfist Ball of Foot
Knifehand   Elbow
        Hand Spear

INNER WRIST

Backfist   Knifehand
Bottomfist Forearm

CHIN

Forefist   Palmheel
Backfist   Elbow
Bottomfist Ball of Foot

CLAVICLES

Bottomfist
Knifehand
Elbow

KIDNEYS

Knifehand   Backfist
Bottomfist Palmheel
Forefist   Elbow

GROIN

Forefist   Elbow
Backfist   Knee
Bottomfist Palmheel
        Ball of Foot

INSTEPS

Heel
Footedge

TEMPLE

Forefist   Elbow
Backfist   Knee
Bottomfist Ball of **Foot**
        Palmheel

BASE OF CEREBELLUM

Bottomfist
Knifehand
Elbow

UPPER BACK

Knifehand
Bottomfist
Elbow

SOLAR PLEXUS

Forefist   Palmheel
Backfist   Elbow
Bottomfist Hand Spear

FLOATING RIBS

Forefist   Palmheel
Backfist   Elbow
        Bottomfist

KNEE CAPS

Ball of Foot
Foot Edge

SHINS

Ball of Foot
Foot Edge
Heel

Chapter Three
AMMUNITION AND TARGET:
Your Anatomy and the
Assailant's

VARIOUS PARTS of your anatomy are useful as striking points—ammunition—against an assailant. In the correct execution of *karate* technique, you must focus your strength into these striking points which makes them more effective than you would expect.

Study your anatomy, thinking of the parts as the powerful striking points you will make them. Carefully note details about fashioning them; that is, the exact method of forming or positioning the striking points.

The hardening or toughening exercises of classical *karate* training which subjects parts of the body to beating and pounding against hard surfaces are *not* essential for effective self-defense. A well-directed blow from an ordinary hand or foot will render an assailant harmless. Board-splitting and stone-cracking belong to the *karate* professional, but even here, such feats are not the object of training. On the other hand, for you the working man, deliberate maiming of your appendages is not socially acceptable, and may be detrimental to your work. Do not suppose that such extremes are essential to an effective *karate* technique.

Everybody, in spite of development and fitness, has certain anatomical weak points. In *karate* you must study these points, noting their exact location, and determine what striking points can best assault them. These weak points are really *vital points*. Consult the chart on page 58.

A variety of effects can be produced by striking different vital points. You must depend upon knowledge of the varying effects in dealing out punishment. Attacking certain vital points causes sharp pain, possible nerve shock, and would probably discourage an ordinary assailant.

This is a minimum form of punishment. A more severe punishment, resulting in severe injury, is possible by increasing the force or your attack by or attacking other vital points. A lethal attack is also possible if *karate* technique is executed against certain vital points. The *karate* exponent, therefore, is able to deal out punishment in varying degrees.

The seriousness of attacking vital points must be constantly in mind and your conduct in any situation must be based on the potential consequences. *Karate* used against an obstreperous person must of necessity be different from the method used against an assailant who is bent on taking your life. Use discretion in attacking vital points.

Use of the Fist: This will be one of your most reliable striking points and perhaps the most commonly used in self-defense. Form it as follows:

1. Starting with your little finger, clench your fingers tightly together by bending only the second and third joints.
2. Roll your fingers tightly into the palm of your hand by bending your finger base knuckles.
3. Anchor your fingers by folding your thumb and pressing it tightly downward against your forefinger and middle finger.

Anytime you use your fist in *karate,* it must be a *tight* fist!

The Forefist: Deliver your fist speedily by following the shortest course open to the target, using the arm on the side of the rearmost leg when you are in the Forward Stance.

Start the tight fist at the hips, palm upward, and drive it forward, twisting the arm inward so that when you strike the target, the palm is pointing downward. Relax the shoulder and keep the wrist and forearm straight as you drive the fist into the target. Simultaneously, the other hand must be withdrawn to the opposite hip, twisting it so that when it comes to rest at the hip, it is in the form of a tight fist, palm upward.

FOCUS the tight fist on the target by twisting the hips to the Front-facing Posture in the direction of the punching action. Strike with the knuckles of the first and second fingers as shown in the sketches.

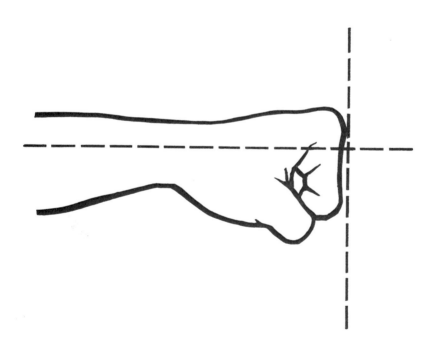

SUGGESTED TARGETS FOR THE FOREFIST

To the face

To the solar plexus

The Back and Bottom Fists: Deliver your fist speedily by using the arm on the side of your advanced leg when you are in the Forward Stance. Strike forward or to the side.

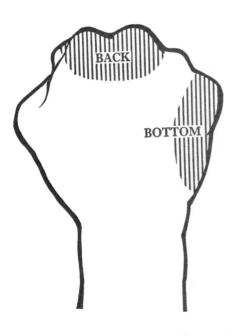
BACK

BOTTOM

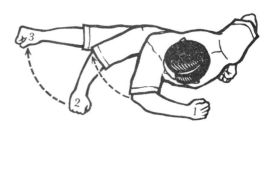

Start your right fist at mid body at any point between the chest and the belt, knuckles upward, arm more or less parallel to the ground. Using the elbow as a pivot point, snap the fist to the target either in an arc over the top, or parallel to the ground, twisting the arm so that the base knuckles of the forefinger and middle finger on the back of the hand strike the target. You may snap the fist to the target in an arc parallel to the ground *without* twisting the arm, so that the *bottom* of the fist strikes the target. In any of these actions keep the other arm close alongside the body, hand held in a tight fist, palm upward at the hip.

FOCUS the tight fist on the target by keeping the wrist and forearm straight and striking either with the back fist, as shown in the pictures, or with the bottom fist (not shown) twisting your hips in the direction of your strike.

SUGGESTED TARGETS FOR BACK and BOTTOM FIST

To the eye

To the chin

To the ribs

Use of the Open Hand: Characteristic of *karate* responses, the open hand serves well in attack or defense situations, used as a striking point to deliver an attack or to block the assailant's offensive action. Form it in one of three ways as follows:

HAND SPEAR

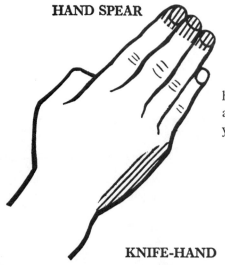

Extend the fingers, tightly together, and hold them in position by folding the thumb and clamping it tightly against the base of your forefinger.

FOR HAND SPEAR USE

1. Keep the hand and forearm in a straight line, making the ends of the three striking fingers flush or nearly so.

FOR KNIFE-HAND USE

KNIFE-HAND

2. Flex the wrist slightly upward toward the back of the hand, concentrating the flex power into the outer edge of the heel of the hand.

FOR PALM-HEEL USE

3. Flex the hand upward toward the back of the hand as far as it will go, palm forward, fingers curled downward at the second joints and thumb pressed tightly against the base knuckle of the forefinger for rigidity.

PALM HEEL

70

The Hand Spear: Deliver the Hand Spear speedily by following the shortest course open to the target. Use the arm on the side of the advanced leg when you are in the Forward Stance. It may also be delivered on the side of the rear leg.

71

The method of delivery is the same as the Forefist (page 61). Only the formation of the hand is different. Start the open hand at the hips, palm upward, and drive it forward, twisting the arm inward so that when you strike the target, the palm is pointing downward. Relax the shoulder and keep the wrist and forearm straight as you drive the Hand Spear into the target. Simultaneously, the other hand must be withdrawn to the opposite hip, twisting it so that it comes to rest at the hip in the form of a Hand Spear or tight fist, palm upward.

Certain targets are better attacked by stopping the twist of your Hand Spear when the thumb is directly upward. The opening to the target determines this.

Both methods should be practiced.

FOCUS the Hand Spear on the target by jabbing the tips of the forefinger, middle finger, and ring finger hard forward, and twisting the hips to the Front-facing Posture in the direction of the thrust.

To the eyes

To the solar plexus

74

The Knife-hand: Deliver the Knife-hand speedily by using the arm on the side of the rearmost leg when you are in the Forward Stance and a Half-front-facing posture.

Start the right Knife-hand in either of two ways—an *outside* or an *inside* delivery depending upon the situation. For the outside delivery, start the open hand, held as a Knife-hand, near the right ear, thumb *down,* elbow pointing to the side and rear. Swing a chopping stroke to the target, twisting the arm so that the knife edge part of the open hand strikes the target. The palm is upward. The other arm is drawn close alongside the body, hand held in a tight fist, palm upward at the hip. (See four pictures at the top of these two pages.)

For the inside delivery, start the open hand, held as a Knife-hand, near the left ear, thumb *up,* elbow pointing forward. Swing a chopping

stroke to the target, twisting the arm so that the knife edge of the open hand strikes the target and the palm is downward. The other arm is drawn close alongside the body, hand held in a tight fist, palm upward at the hip. (See four pictures at bottom.)

FOCUS either Knife-hand on the target by twisting the hips in the direction of the striking action and using a bent arm action to give a chopping style of delivery. Do not strike the target with a perfectly straightened arm. Follow the pictures for correct form.

SUGGESTED TARGETS FOR THE KNIFE-HAND

To the **neck**

To the ear

The Palm-heel: Deliver the Palm-heel speedily by following the shortest course open to the target, using the arm on the side of the rearmost leg when you are in the Forward Stance, though sometimes it may be delivered on the side of the advanced leg.

The method of delivery is much like a punching action with a fist, but in place of a fist, the hand is formed as a Palm-heel. Start the Palm-heel, palm upward from a low position, and drive it forward and upward, jutting the heel of the open hand hard into the target. The other hand is withdrawn close to the body, twisting it so that it comes to rest at the hip in the form of a tight fist, palm upward. An alternate lateral delivery of the Palm-heel is shown in the lower three pictures and requires a simple snapping action of the wrist. This can also be applied in a downward or upward direction. (See pictures page 46.)

FOCUS the Palm-heel on the target by twisting the hips in the direction of the thrusting action and snapping the heel of the open hand with a slightly bent arm as you strike.

To the chin

Use of the Elbow: The elbow, equally desirable for frontal or rear attack situations, is strong, fast, and effective and is a sure means of stopping an assailant when properly used. Form it as follows:

Bend the arm so that you expose the prominent bone at the elbow. The elbow should not be completely rigid.

The Elbow Sideward Strike: Deliver the elbow speedily by following the shortest course to the target, using the arm on the side of the advanced leg when you are in the Forward Stance and Half-front-facing Posture. Start the elbow from across the body with that hand at the farthest breast, in a tight fist, knuckles downward. Drive elbow sideward, twisting the arm inward so that as you strike the target the palm is pointing downward. This line of direction is close to your body. Simultaneously, withdraw the other hand to the opposite hip, twisting it so that as it comes to rest at the hip, it is in the form of a tight fist, palm upward. See the four pictures at the top of these two pages.

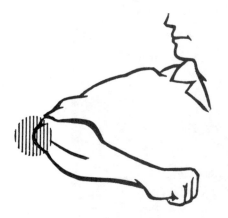

FOCUS the elbow on the target by keeping the wrist and forearm straight, and twist the hips to the Front-facing Posture as you strike the target.

The Elbow Forward Strike: Deliver the elbow speedily by following the shortest course to the target, using the arm on the side of the rear-most leg when you are in the Forward Stance and Half-front-facing Posture. Start the elbow from alongside the body with that hand in a tight fist, knuckles downward. Drive the arm forward, pointing the elbow at the target, twisting the arm inward so that as you strike, the palm is pointing downward. The line of direction is close to the body and straight toward the target, *not* looping or in an arc. Simultaneously, withdraw the other hand to the opposite hip, twisting it so that as it comes to rest at the hip, it is in the form of a tight fist, palm upward. See four pictures at the bottom of these two pages.

FOCUS the elbow on the target by keeping the wrist and the forearm straight. Twist the hips to the Front-facing Posture as you strike the target. Do not lift the shoulder of the striking arm as you drive the elbow forward.

The Elbow Upward Strike: Deliver the elbow speedily by following the shortest course open to the target, using the arm on the side of the rearmost leg when you are in the Forward Stance and Half-front-facing Posture. Start the elbow at the side close alongside the body, hand held in a tight fist, palm upward. Drive the elbow forward and upward, twisting the arm slightly so that the palm is turned inward and the fist comes to rest near the ear on the side of the striking elbow. Simultaneously, withdraw the other hand to the opposite hip, twisting it so that as it comes to rest at the hip, it is in the form of a tight fist, palm upward. See four pictures across the top of these two pages.

FOCUS the elbow on the target by slightly dropping the hips and twisting them to the Front-facing Posture as you strike the target.

The Elbow Downward Strike: Deliver the elbow speedily by following the shortest course open to the target, using the arm on either the advanced (not shown) or rearmost leg when you are in the Forward Stance and Half-front-facing Posture. Start the elbow from as high as you can reach without breaking your stability. Hold the hand of the striking arm in a tight fist. Drive the elbow downward, twisting the arm inward so that as you strike the target the palm is facing you. This line of direction is close to the body. Simultaneously, withdraw the other hand to the opposite hip, twisting it so that as it comes to rest at the hip, it is in the form of a tight fist, palm upward.

FOCUS the elbow on the target by slightly dropping the hips and twisting them to the Front-facing Posture as you strike the target.

To the solar plexus, face, or ribs

To the base of the neck

Use of the Foot: A properly delivered *karate* kick is more powerful than any other blow you can generate. For the most part, your shoes will be the points of contact, but you must carefully practice kicking responses in order to become effective in frontal and rear attack situations.

Improper kicking will get you in trouble. Loss of balance, your kicking leg being grabbed by the assailant, and other dangers may result in serious consequences. Unless you are quite flexible and athletically inclined, it is best that you limit kicking to groin level or lower. Form the foot in three ways as follows:

1. Curl the toes upward as far as possible inside the shoe. Flex the ankle upward, slightly concentrating the flex power into the ball of the foot for frontal kicking. (See top drawing.)

or

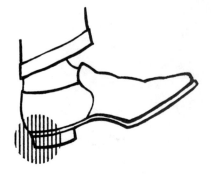

2. Flex the ankle upward, slightly concentrating the flex power into the heel of the foot for rear stamping or kicking. (See middle drawing.)

or

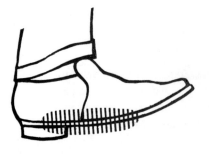

3. Flex the ankle sideward by turning the sole inward and concentrating the flex power into the outer edge of the foot nearest the heel for side thrust kicking. (See bottom drawing.)

The Ball of the Foot: Deliver the ball of the foot speedily by following the shortest course to the target, kicking directly to the front of your body, using the rearmost leg when you are in the Forward Stance.

Start the kick by bending the kicking leg and lifting that knee so that the thigh is parallel to the ground, toes pointing toward the target. Keep weighted leg slightly bent with the heel on the ground. Snap the leg forward, pivoting on the knee joint so that the ball of the foot strikes the target. (See drawing on page 90.)

Immediately allow the kicking leg to return to the position where the thigh is parallel to the ground *before* returning it to its original position in the Forward Stance. During this action, the arms remain free to aid in body balance. Unless you are unusually limber, it is best to keep the target at groin level or lower.

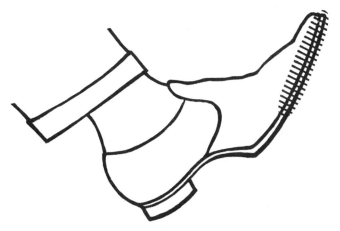

FOCUS the ball of the foot on the target by thrusting the hips slightly forward and the upper body slightly backward as you snap into the target. The ankle and knee joints of the support leg must be fixed during the kicking action to maintain balance and to allow a strong kicking attack.

To the shin, knee, groin, or abdominal region

The Heel: Deliver the heel speedily to the target by following the shortest course open to the target, using the rearmost leg when you are in the Forward Stance.

Start the stamping action by bringing the thigh parallel to the ground and flexing the foot upward toward the shin, thus jutting the heel downward. The support leg must remain slightly bent at the knee but fixed tightly at the ankle and knee joints. Drive the stamping leg directly to the target by thrusting and stamping the heel straight downward so that the sharp part of the heel strikes the target. Immediately withdraw the stamping leg to a bent-knee position and return it to the ground in a Forward Stance. Using the heel of the foot in a thrusting action parallel to the ground is generally not advisable, unless you are unusually flexible.

FOCUS the heel of the foot on target by keeping your balance on the support leg and fixing the hips to provide a stable base for the stamping action.

To the instep

The Foot Edge: Deliver the edge of the foot speedily by following the shortest course to the target, using the rearmost leg when you are in the Forward Stance.

Start the kick by bringing the thigh parallel to the ground, knee bent, and the side of the foot facing the target. The support leg must remain slightly bent at the knee, but fixed tightly at the ankle and knee joints. Drive the kicking leg directly to the target by thrusting the leg sideways in a straight line so that the edge of the foot strikes the target. Immediately withdraw the kicking leg to the bent-knee position in front of the body and return to the Forward Stance. During this action, the arms remain free to aid body balance.

FOCUS the edge of the foot on the target by thrusting the hips *slightly* sideward in the direction of the kick. Lean the upper body slightly sideways, opposite to the kick, as you thrust into the target. The ankle and knee joints of the support leg must be fixed during the kicking action to maintain balance and to apply a strong kicking attack.

To the knee or shin

Use of the Knee: Reliable in close-in fighting, the knee is a powerful striking point which should not be overlooked in *karate* self-defense training.

The knee can only be applied to frontal attacks with facility and is formed as follows:

Bend the leg sufficiently so that you expose the prominent point of the knee cap. The leg must not be rigid.

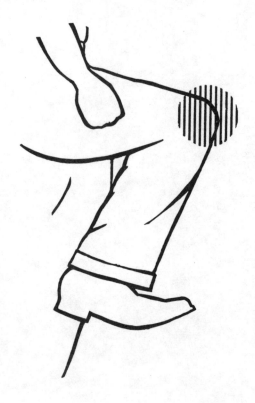

The Front Knee Kick: Deliver the knee speedily by following the shortest course open to the target, using the rearmost leg when you are in the Forward Stance. The lead leg may be used in some cases.

Start the kneeing action by swinging the knee, point first, upward. The support leg must remain slightly bent at the knee, but fixed tightly at the ankle and knee joints. Smash the knee directly into the target in a straight line so that the point of the knee strikes the target. Immediately withdraw the kneeing leg and return it to its former position on the ground. Using the knee in a "roundhouse" fashion is difficult and, unless you are unusually flexible, not advisable.

FOCUS the knee on the target by keeping the balance on the support leg and fixing the hips to provide a stable base for the kneeing action. The ankle of the support leg must be fixed during this action. The back is more or less straight at the moment of impact with the target.

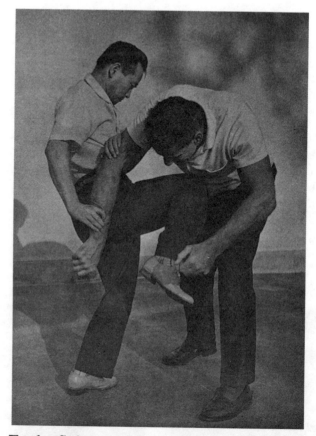

To the Solar plexus or groin

ALTHOUGH this volume is designed for the individual interested in self-defense and has, therefore, been modified to fit the needs and capabilities of the average man, the pictures on this and the following pages show several karate techniques in their pure and exciting classical form.